WHY DO I VOMIT?

BY Emilie Dufresne

THE SECRET BOOK COMPANY

©2019
The Secret Book Company
King's Lynn
Norfolk PE30 4LS

All facts, statistics, web addresses and URLs in this book were verified as valid and accurate at time of writing.
No responsibility for any changes to external websites or references can be accepted by either the author or publisher.

All rights reserved.
Printed in Malaysia.

A catalogue record for this book is available from the British Library.

ISBN: 978-1-78998-046-2

Written by:
Emilie Dufresne

Edited by:
Kirsty Holmes

Designed by:
Danielle Rippengill

IMAGE CREDITS

CONTENTS

Words that look like **this** can be found in the glossary on page 24.

ARE YOU FEELING QUEASY?

Sometimes, our stomachs start to feel funny... and we feel something rising in our bodies...

GULP!

Then we... VOMIT!

4

But why and how does this happen? There are lots of different things that might make us vomit. Here are some examples.

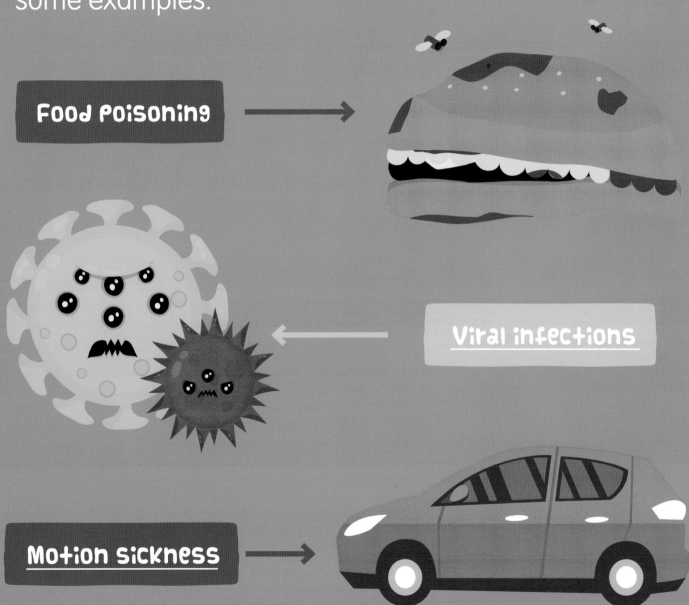

Food poisoning

Viral infections

Motion sickness

GAGGING AND RETCHING

Before we actually vomit, we might gag or retch. This is where the **muscles** inside our body **contract** and **relax** over and over again.

Stomach

This makes anything inside your stomach move around quickly.

Sometimes we can gag and retch and not be sick. This might happen because we have seen or smelt something really gross.

Sometimes seeing someone else vomit can make us want to vomit as well!

DIGESTION GONE WRONG

The digestive system usually moves food downwards through your body, **filtering** all the **nutrients** from your food. But when you are going to vomit, everything goes a bit topsy-turvy...

Start at stage 1 and follow the vomit all the way back up the body!

STAGE 3:

The sick then comes out of your **MOUTH** – with a top speed of around 18 metres per second!

STAGE 2: Then it is pushed out of the **STOMACH** and into the **OESOPHAGUS (SAY: UH-SOFF-A-GUS)**...

STAGE 1: First, anything in your **INTESTINES** is pushed back into the stomach...

FOOD POISONING

We can get food poisoning from eating food that has gone off, or food that has been **contaminated** with bad **bacteria**.

Our bodies will do everything they can to get the bad food out.

Food poisoning might make us vomit lots, have diarrhoea **(SAY: DIE-AH-REE-AH)** or have a temperature. These will either kill the bad bacteria or get them out of our bodies.

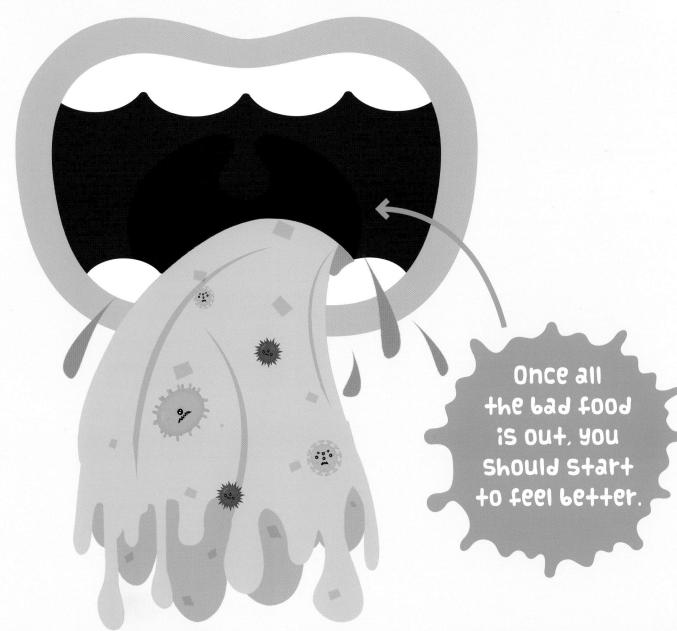

Once all the bad food is out, you should start to feel better.

VIRUSES

Viral infections, such as stomach flu, are highly **contagious** and can make us vomit – a lot!

ON

OFF

Stomach viruses are easily passed from person to person. Always make sure you wash your hands!

When we are sick, contagious **particles** are spread far and wide. Scientists even made a robot called Vomiting Larry to show just how far these particles travel.

Check out Vomiting Larry in action here!
www.bbc.co.uk/science/0/21149223

Larry vomited one litre of fluid over a distance of nearly eight metres squared!

THEME PARK PUKE

If we go on a rollercoaster or travel in a car, train or plane, then we might feel (or even be) sick. This is because of motion sickness.

If we can feel movement, but our eyes can't see that we are moving (or the other way round), our bodies get confused – and feel sick!

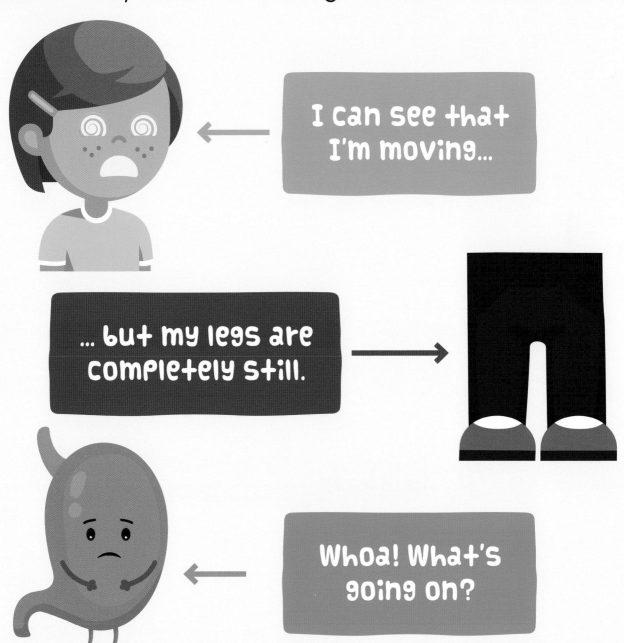

SORE THROATS AND BLOCKED NOSES

When we vomit, the sick can come out of both our mouths and our noses. This is because the oesophagus is connected to both your nose and your mouth.

Sometimes sick is travelling so fast, it has to come out of both the nose and mouth!

When we vomit, everything in our stomach and intestines is thrown up, including the acid that is used to break down food.

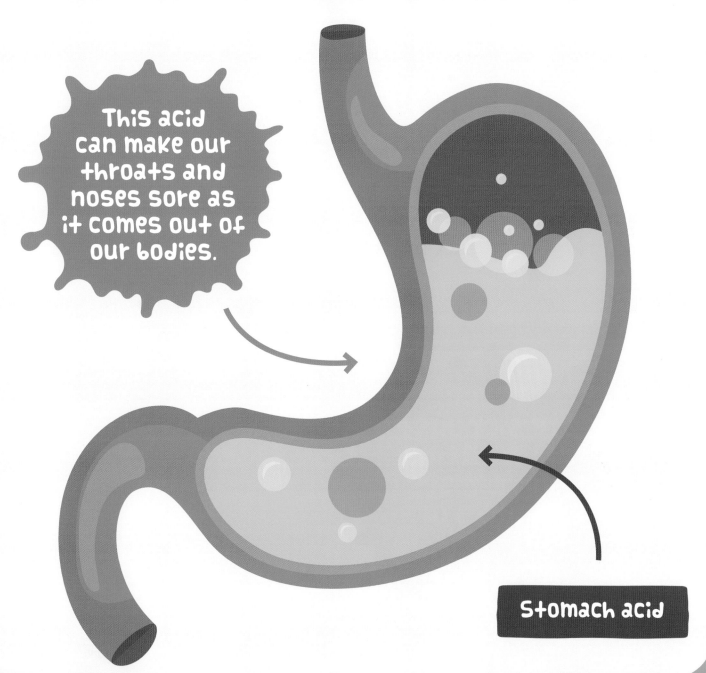

FUNKY AND CHUNKY

Vomit can be different colours and different textures depending on what we eat or drink and how digested our food is.

If you are sick just after eating, you will see chunks of that food in your sick.

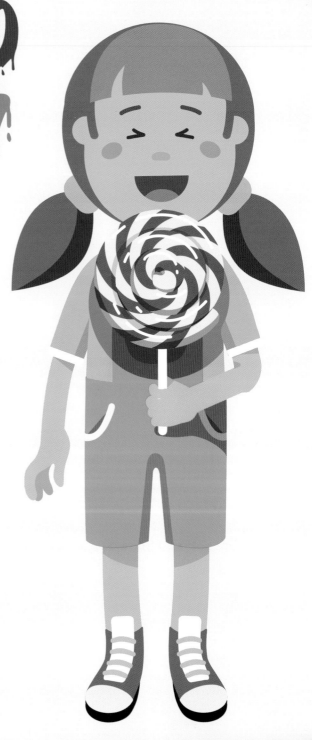

For example, if you have just eaten a red lolly and then you are sick, your vomit will probably have bits of red lolly in it!

If you haven't eaten at all, you might vomit a bitter, yellow liquid. This is called bile.

19

SICK STUFF

Parmesan cheese and vomit smell very similar because they both contain the same type of acid.

PEW!

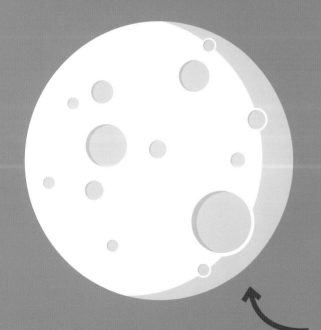

There is vomit on the moon because some astronauts left their sick bags there!

If a dog is sick, they might eat their own vomit. They use their excellent sense of smell to find tasty bits of food left in it!

People can have a fear of vomiting or seeing other people vomit. This is called emetophobia.

ACTIVITY

Can you match the food with the vomit?

A.

B.

C.

D.

GLOSSARY

bacteria	microscopic living things that can cause diseases
contagious	(of a disease) able to spread from one person to another
contaminated	to have made something unclean by adding a poisonous or polluting substance to it
contract	(of muscles) to become shorter or smaller through tightening
filtering	removing unwanted materials by passing through something, like a sieve
metres squared	a measurement of an area that is a square with each side being a metre in length
motion sickness	feeling sick or nauseous while travelling or moving
muscles	bundles of tissue that can contract or squeeze together
nutrients	natural substances that people need to grow and stay healthy
particles	extremely small pieces of a substance
relax	(of muscles) to become longer and bigger by not being tensed
viral infections	illnesses that are caused by a virus being inside the body

INDEX